Warner Juvenile Books Edition

Warner Books, Inc., 666 Fifth Avenue, New York, NY 10103
A Warner Communications Company

Printed in the United States of America
First Warner Juvenile Books Printing: October 1988
10 9 8 7 6 5 4 3 2 1

Library of Congress Cataloging-in-Publication Data

Gilchrist, Guy.
Guy Gilchrist's tiny dinos big and small: a book of opposites.
p. cm.

Summary: Rex, Bronty, and the other tiny dinos demonstrate opposite qualities, such as up and down, wet and dry, and new and old.
[1. English, language – Synonyms and antonyms – Fiction. 2. Dinosaurs – Fiction. 3. Stories in rhyme.] I. Title. II. Title: Tiny dinos big and small.
PZ8.3.G39Tim 1988 88-12097
[E] – dc19
ISBN 1-55782-106-2

FOR DOWNTOWN ELLEN BROWN!

Guy Gilchrist's

TINY DINOS

BIG AND SMALL

A BOOK OF OPPOSITES

WARNER JUVENILE BOOKS
A Warner Communications Company
NEW YORK

"I am BIG!"
Rex says to Tort.
"And you are
SMALL! SMALL! SMALL!"

"Here comes Bronty,"
says LITTLE Tort.
"She's the BIGGEST
of us all!"

"I am TALL," says Bronty.
"To *me*, Rex, you are SHORT.
If I were you, I'd remember that
before you pick on Tort!"

Tiny Ptery is UP
and Steggie is DOWN....

She's in the air.
He's on the ground.

The island rain
falls from the sky.
Now Ptery's WET
but Steggie's DRY.

"GO! GO! GO!" yells Plateo.
"I love to move! I love to GO!"

"You cannot GO! You have to STOP!
This sign says so!" says the monkey cop.

"Look at me!" says Triceratot.
"I'm all dressed up and Bronty's not!
My dress is NEW
and hers is OLD!"

"Yes," says Bronty…
"so I'm told."

"I'm hungry," says Rex,
"so don't think I'm rude
if I pig out a little
and eat all your food!!!"

"That's okay," says Plateo,
"if you do that.
'Cause I'll stay THIN
and you'll stay FAT!"

Tiny Dinos big and small,
short and fat and thin and tall.
They are quite different,
all different, you see,
but they all live together
in one family.

THE JOLLY TURTLE

easy

Cocktails

easy
Cocktails

LOVE FOOD

First published in 2009
Love Food ® is an imprint of Parragon Books Ltd

Parragon
Queen Street House
4 Queen Street
Bath BA1 1HE, UK

ISBN: 978-1-4075-7557-5

Photography by Mike Cooper
Food Styling by Lincoln Jefferson and Carole Handslip
Introduction text by Linda Doeser

Printed in China

NOTES FOR THE READER

This book uses imperial, metric, and US cup measurements. Follow the same units of measurement throughout; do not mix imperial and metric. All spoon measurements are level: teaspoons are assumed to be 5 ml, and tablespoons are assumed to be 15 ml. Unless otherwise stated, milk is assumed to be whole, eggs are medium, and pepper is freshly ground black pepper.

Recipes using raw or very lightly cooked eggs should be avoided by infants, the elderly, pregnant women, convalescents, and anyone with a chronic condition. Pregnant and breastfeeding women are advised to avoid eating peanuts and peanut products. People with nut allergies should be aware that some of the prepared ingredients used in the recipes in this book may contain nuts. Always check the packaging before use.

Please drink alcohol responsibly.

Contents

Introduction

Cocktails drift in and out of fashion but their appeal is always to the young, or at least the young at heart. Making mixed drinks—even the wonderfully colorful and exotic concoctions of the contemporary cocktail bar—isn't difficult and is a lot of fun. Reading the following basic guidelines should guarantee that you have all the skills of a professional bartender at your fingertips.

Bar Essentials

Cocktail shaker: The standard type is a cylindrical metal container with a capacity of 2¼ cups that has a double lid incorporating a perforated strainer. To use, remove the lid, add ice, and pour in the ingredients listed in the recipe. Close securely and shake vigorously for 10–20 seconds, until the outside of the shaker is frosted with a fine mist. Remove the small lid and pour the cocktail into the appropriate glass. If your cocktail shaker doesn't have a built-in strainer, you will need a separate one. The Boston shaker consists of double conical containers and is designed to be used with a Hawthorn strainer. It's best not to mix more than 2 servings at a time.

Mixing glass: This is used for making clear cocktails. It need be no more complicated than the container of your cocktail shaker or a pitcher about the same size, but you can also buy a professional mixing glass. To use, add ice, pour in the ingredients listed in the recipe, and stir vigorously for 20 seconds. Strain into the appropriate glass.

Strainer: A bar strainer or Hawthorn strainer is the perfect tool to prevent ice and other unwanted ingredients from being poured from the shaker or mixing glass into the serving glass. You can also use a small nylon strainer.

Jigger: This small measuring cup is often double-ended and shaped like an hourglass. A standard measure is 1½ fluid ounces (3 tbsp). Most jiggers have a 1½-fluid ounces cup on one end and a ¾-fluid ounces cup on the other. The proportions of the various ingredients are critical, not the specific quantities, so if you don't have a jigger, you can use the small lid of your cocktail shaker, a liqueur, schnapps, or shot glass, or even a small eggcup.

Bar spoon: This long-handled spoon is used for stirring cocktails in a mixing glass.

Muddler: This is simply a miniature masher used for crushing ingredients, such as herbs and sugar, in the bottom of a glass. You can also use a mortar and pestle or even the back of a spoon.

Other basics: A lot of ordinary kitchen equipment is useful: 1 or more corkscrews, citrus juicer or reamer, cutting board, paring and kitchen knives, citrus zester, a selection of pitchers, measuring cups, and a blender for creamy cocktails and slushes. You will also need an ice bucket and tongs—never pick up ice with your fingers. Optional extras include swizzle sticks and straws.

Glasses

Balloon wine glass: Short-stemmed glass with a large bowl holding 10 fluid ounces.

Champagne flute: Tall thin glass holding 4–5 fluid ounces.

Cocktail glass: Stemmed glass with a cone-shaped bowl holding 4–5 fluid ounces.

Collins glass: Tall narrow glass with straight sides holding 10 oz.

Highball glass: Tall straight glass holding 8 oz.

Margarita glass: Stemmed glass with a small bowl topped with a wide saucer shape.

Old-fashioned glass: Chunky glass holding 8 oz.

Shot glass: Small glass holding 2 fluid ounces suitable for shooters.

Bartender's Tips

Sugar syrup: Even superfine sugar often fails to dissolve completely in the brief time that a cocktail is shaken or stirred, so it is better to use sugar syrup when sweetening drinks. To make this, put 4 tablespoons of superfine sugar and 4 tablespoons of water into a small pan. Gradually bring to a boil over low heat, stirring constantly, until the sugar has dissolved. Boil, without stirring, for 1–2 minutes, then remove from the heat and let cool. Store in a sterilized jar or bottle in the refrigerator for up to 2 months.

Chilling: For absolute perfection, you should chill spirits, mixers, and serving glasses in the refrigerator. However, it's not always possible to find room for glasses and you should never put fine crystal in the refrigerator. As an alternative, fill glasses with cracked ice, stir well, then spill out the ice and any water before pouring in the cocktail.

Frosting glasses: You can use superfine sugar, fine salt, or dry unsweetened coconut to decorate the rim of a glass. Rub the rim with a little lemon or lime juice and then dip the glass upside down into a shallow saucer of your chosen decoration.

Layering pousse-café: To make a multilayered drink, slowly pour the liqueurs or spirits, in the order specified in the recipe, over the back of a teaspoon into the glass. Each layer then settles on top of the layer before it.

Ice: To crack ice, put cubes in a strong plastic bag and hit with the smooth side of a meat mallet or a rolling pin. Alternatively, bang the bag against a wall. To store large quantities of ice, place the cubes in a strong plastic bag and before returning them to the freezer squirt with club soda to stop the cubes from sticking together.

1

Cool Classics

Cosmopolitan

Serves 1

2 measures vodka

1 measure triple sec

1 measure fresh lime juice

1 measure cranberry juice

ice

orange peel, to decorate

Shake all the liquid ingredients over ice until well frosted.

Strain into a chilled cocktail glass.

Dress with the strip of orange peel.

Daiquiri

Serves 1

2 measures white rum

3/4 measure lime juice

1/2 tsp sugar syrup

cracked ice

Pour the rum, lime juice, and sugar syrup over ice and shake vigorously until well frosted.

Strain into a chilled cocktail glass.

Manhattan

Serves 1

dash Angostura bitters

3 measures rye whiskey

1 measure sweet vermouth

cracked ice

cocktail cherry, to decorate

Shake the liquids over cracked ice in a mixing glass and mix well.

Strain into a chilled glass and decorate with the cherry.

Sangria

Serves 6

juice 1 orange

juice 1 lemon

2 tbsp confectioners' sugar

ice cubes

1 orange, thinly sliced

1 lemon, thinly sliced

1 bottle red wine, chilled

lemon-flavor soda pop

Shake the orange and lemon juices with the sugar, and transfer to a large bowl or pitcher.

When the sugar has dissolved, add a few ice cubes, the sliced fruit, and wine.

Marinate for 1 hour if possible, and then add the lemon-flavor soda pop to taste and more ice.

Mimosa

Serves 1

flesh 1 passion fruit

½ measure orange curaçao

crushed ice

champagne, chilled

star fruit slice, to decorate

Scoop out the passion fruit flesh into a pitcher or shaker and shake with the curaçao and a little crushed ice until frosted.

Pour into the bottom of a champagne flute and fill with champagne.

Dress with the slice of star fruit.

Margarita

Serves 1

lime wedge

coarse salt

3 measures white tequila

1 measure triple sec or Cointreau

2 measures lime juice

cracked ice

lime wedge, to decorate

Rub the rim of a chilled cocktail glass with the lime wedge and then dip in a saucer of coarse salt to frost.

Put the cracked ice into a cocktail shaker. Pour the tequila, triple sec, and lime juice over the ice. Shake vigorously until a frost forms.

Strain into the prepared glass and dress with the wedge of lime.

Club Mojito

Serves 1

1 tsp sugar syrup
few mint leaves, plus extra to decorate
juice ½ lime
ice
2 measures Jamaican rum
club water
dash Angostura bitters

Put the syrup, mint leaves, and lime juice in a cocktail glass and crush or muddle the mint leaves.

Add ice and rum, then fill with club soda to taste.

Finish with a dash of Angostura bitters and the mint leaves.

Mai Tai

Serves 1

2 measures white rum

2 measures dark rum

1 measure orange Curaçao

1 measure lime juice

1 tbsp orgeat

1 tbsp grenadine

cracked ice

pineapple slices, fruit peel pieces, cocktail cherries, and straws, to decorate

Shake the white and dark rums, Curaçao, lime juice, orgeat, and grenadine vigorously over ice until well frosted.

Strain into a chilled cocktail glass and dress as you like.

Woo-Woo

Serves 1

cracked ice
2 measures vodka
2 measures peach schnapps
4 measures cranberry juice
peach slice, to decorate

Fill a chilled cocktail glass halfway with cracked ice.

Pour the vodka, peach schnapps, and cranberry juice over the ice.

Stir well to mix and dress with the peach slice.

Mint Julep

Serves 1

leaves from 1 fresh mint sprig, plus an extra sprig, to decorate

1 tbsp sugar syrup

crushed ice

3 measures bourbon whiskey

Put the mint leaves and sugar syrup into a small chilled glass and mash with a teaspoon.

Add the crushed ice and shake to mix before adding the bourbon.

Dress with the mint sprig.

Whiskey Sour

Serves 1

1 measure lemon or lime juice

2 measures blended whiskey

1 tsp confectioners' sugar or sugar syrup

ice

lime or lemon slice, to decorate

maraschino cherry, to decorate

Shake the lemon juice, whiskey, and sugar well over ice and strain into a cocktail glass.

Dress with the slice of lime or lemon and the cherry.

Martini

Serves 1

3 measures gin

1 tsp dry vermouth, or to taste

cracked ice

green cocktail olive, to decorate

Pour the gin and vermouth over cracked ice in a mixing glass and stir well to mix.

Strain into a chilled cocktail glass and dress with the cocktail olive.

Sex on the Beach

Serves 1

1 measure peach schnapps

1 measure vodka

2 measures fresh orange juice

3 measures cranberry and peach juice

ice and crushed ice

dash lemon juice

orange peel piece, to decorate

Shake the peach schnapps, vodka, orange juice, and cranberry and peach juice over ice until well frosted.

Strain into a glass filled with crushed ice and squeeze on the lemon juice.

Dress with the orange peel.

Harvey Wallbanger

Serves 1

ice cubes

3 measures vodka

8 measures orange juice

2 tsp Galliano

cherry and orange slice, to decorate

Fill a tall glass halfway with ice, pour the vodka and orange juice over the ice cubes, and float Galliano on top.

Dress with the cherry and slice of orange.

For a warming variant, mix a splash of ginger wine with the vodka and orange.

Bloody Mary

Serves 1

dash Worcestershire sauce
dash Tabasco sauce
cracked ice
2 measures vodka
splash dry sherry
6 measures tomato juice
juice ½ lemon
pinch celery salt
pinch cayenne pepper
celery stalk with leaves, to decorate
lemon slice, to decorate

Dash the Worcestershire sauce and Tabasco sauce over ice in a shaker and add the vodka, splash of dry sherry, tomato juice, and lemon juice.

Shake vigorously until frosted.

Strain into a tall chilled glass, add a pinch of celery salt and a pinch of cayenne, and dress with the celery stalk and the slice of lemon.

Slow Comfortable Screw

Serves 1

2 measures sloe gin
orange juice
cracked ice cubes
orange slice, to decorate

Shake the sloe gin and orange juice over ice until well frosted and pour into a chilled glass.

Dress with the slice of orange.

Long Island Iced Tea

Serves 1

2 measures vodka

1 measure gin

1 measure white tequila

1 measure white rum

½ measure white crème de menthe

2 measures lemon juice

1 tsp sugar syrup

cracked ice

cola

lime or lemon wedge, to decorate

Shake the vodka, gin, tequila, rum, crème de menthe, lemon juice, and sugar syrup vigorously over ice until well frosted.

Strain into an ice-filled tall glass and fill with cola.

Dress with the lime or lemon wedge.

2

Small but Mighty

Tequila Slammer

Serves 1

1 measure white tequila, chilled

1 measure lemon juice

sparkling wine, chilled

Put the tequila and lemon juice into a chilled glass.

Fill with sparkling wine.

Cover the glass with your hand, slam, and drink.

B-52

Serves 1

1 measure chilled dark crème de cacao

1 measure chilled Baileys Irish Cream

1 measure chilled Grand Marnier

Pour the dark crème de cacao into a shot glass.

With a steady hand, gently pour in the chilled Baileys Irish Cream to make a second layer, then gently pour in the chilled Grand Marnier.

Pousse-Café

Serves 1

1/4 measure grenadine

1/4 measure crème de menthe

1/4 measure Galliano

1/4 measure kümmel

1/4 measure brandy

Ice all the liqueurs and a tall shot, elgin, or pousse-café glass.

Carefully pour the liqueurs over a spoon evenly into the glass.

Let stand for a few minutes to settle.

Perfect Love

Serves 1

1 measure vodka

½ measure Parfait Amour

½ measure maraschino liqueur

crushed ice

Shake all the liquid ingredients together over ice until frosted.

Strain into a chilled, tall thin glass with more ice.

Voodoo

Serves 1

½ measure chilled Kahlúa

½ measure chilled Malibu

½ measure chilled butterscotch schnapps

1 measure chilled milk

Pour the Kahlúa, Malibu, schnapps, and milk into a glass and stir well.

Zipper

Serves 1

crushed ice

1 measure tequila

½ measure Grand Marnier

½ measure light cream

Put the crushed ice into a cocktail shaker and pour in the tequila, Grand Marnier, and cream.

Close the shaker and shake vigorously for 10–20 seconds, until the outside of the shaker is misted. Strain into a shot glass.

Wobbly Margarita Shot

Serves 10

½ lime, cut into wedges

2 tbsp fine salt

1 envelope lime gelatin

1 cup hot water

4 tbsp Cointreau

scant 1 cup tequila

Rub the outside rims of 8 shot glasses with the lime wedges, then dip in the salt to frost them. Set aside.

Place the gelatin in a large heatproof measuring pitcher. Pour in the hot water and stir until the gelatin has dissolved. Let cool, then stir in the Cointreau and tequila to make the mixture up to 2 cups. Divide among the prepared shot glasses, being careful not to disturb the salt frosting, and chill in the refrigerator until set.

Jealousy

Serves 1

1 tsp crème de menthe

1–2 tbsp heavy cream

2 measures coffee or chocolate liqueur

chocolate sticks, to serve

Gently beat the mint liqueur into the cream until thick.

Pour the coffee liqueur into a very small iced glass and carefully spoon on the whipped flavored cream.

Serve with the chocolate sticks.

Napoleon's Nightcap

Serves 1

1¼ measures cognac

1 measure dark crème de cacao

¼ measure crème de banane

ice

1 tbsp cream

Stir the cognac, crème de cacao, and crème de banane in a mixing glass with ice.

Strain into a chilled glass and spoon on a layer of cream.

Toffee Split

Serves 1

crushed ice

2 measures Drambuie

1 measure toffee liqueur, iced

Fill a small cocktail glass or shot glass with crushed ice.

Pour on the Drambuie and pour in the toffee liqueur carefully from the side of the glass so it layers on top.

Drink immediately.

Tequila Shot

Serves 1

1 measure gold tequila

pinch salt

lime wedge

Pour the tequila into a shot glass.

Put the salt at the bottom of your thumb, between your thumb and index finger.

Hold the lime wedge in the same hand.

Hold the shot in the other hand.

Lick the salt, down the tequila, and suck the lime.

After Five

Serves 1

½ measure chilled peppermint schnapps

1 measure chilled Kahlúa

1 tbsp chilled Baileys Irish Cream

Pour the peppermint schnapps into a shot glass. Carefully pour the Kahlúa over the back of a teaspoon so that it forms a separate layer. Finally, float the Baileys Irish Cream on top.

Aurora Borealis

Serves 1

1 measure iced grappa or vodka

1 measure iced green Chartreuse

½ measure iced orange Curaçao

few drops iced cassis

Pour the grappa slowly around one side of a well-chilled shot glass.

Gently pour the Chartreuse around the other side.

Pour the Curaçao gently into the middle and add a few drops of cassis just before serving. Don't stir. Drink slowly!

African Mint

Serves 1

¾ measure crème de menthe, chilled

¾ measure Amarula, chilled

Pour the crème de menthe into the bottom of a slim cocktail glass or shot glass, saving a few drops.

Pour the Amarula slowly over the back of a spoon to create a layer over the crème de menthe.

Drizzle any remaining drops of crème de menthe over the creamy liqueur to finish.

Cowboy

Serves 1

3 measures rye whiskey
2 tbsp half-and-half cream
cracked ice

Pour the whiskey and half-and-half over ice and shake vigorously until well frosted.

Strain into a chilled glass.

Nuclear Fallout

Serves 1

1 tsp raspberry syrup

¼ measure maraschino liqueur

¼ measure yellow Chartreuse

¼ measure Cointreau

½ measure well-iced blue curaçao

Chill all the liqueurs but put the blue curaçao in the coldest part of the freezer. Also chill a shot or pousse-café glass.

Carefully pour the liqueurs except the blue curaçao in layers over the back of a teaspoon.

Finally, pour in the blue curaçao and wait for the fallout!

Alabama Slammer

Serves 1

1 measure Southern Comfort

1 measure amaretto

½ measure sloe gin

½ tsp lemon juice

Pour the Southern Comfort, amaretto, and sloe gin over cracked ice in a mixing glass and stir.

Strain into a shot glass and add the lemon juice.

Cover and slam.

Brain Hemorrhage

Serves 1

1 measure chilled peach schnapps

1 tsp chilled Baileys Irish Cream

½ tsp chilled grenadine

Pour the peach schnapps into a shot glass, then carefully float the Baileys on top. Finally, fill with the grenadine.

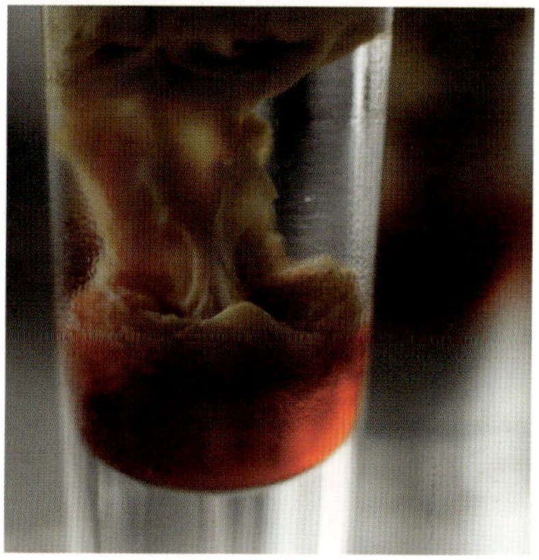

3

Something Different

Vodkatini

Serves 1

1 measure vodka

ice

dash dry vermouth

lemon peel twist, to decorate

Pour the vodka over a handful of ice in a mixing glass.

Add the vermouth, stir well, and strain into a cocktail glass.

Dress with the twist of lemon peel.

Spotted Bikini

Serves 1

2 measures vodka

1 measure white rum

1 measure cold milk

juice 1/2 lemon

ice

1 ripe passion fruit

lemon peel slice, to decorate

Shake the vodka, white rum, milk, and lemon juice over ice until well frosted.

Strain into a chilled cocktail glass and at the last minute add the passion fruit, not strained, so you see the black seeds.

Dress with the slice of lemon peel.

Peartini

Serves 1

1 tsp superfine sugar

pinch ground cinnamon

1 lemon wedge

cracked ice

1 measure vodka

1 measure pear brandy, such as Poire William or Pera Segnana

Combine the sugar and cinnamon on a saucer. Rub the outside rim of a cocktail glass with the lemon wedge, then dip it into the sugar-and-cinnamon mixture. Set aside.

Put the cracked ice into a mixing glass or pitcher and pour in the vodka and pear brandy. Stir well and strain into the prepared glass, without disturbing the frosting.

Vodka Espresso

Serves 1

cracked ice

2 measures espresso or other strong brewed coffee, cooled

1 measure vodka

2 tsp superfine sugar

1 measure Amarula

Put the cracked ice into a cocktail shaker, pour in the coffee and vodka, and add the sugar.

Cover and shake vigorously for 10–20 seconds, until the outside of the shaker is misted.

Strain into a cocktail glass, then float the Amarula on top.

Flirtini

Serves 1

1/4 slice fresh pineapple, chopped

1/2 measure chilled Cointreau

1/2 measure chilled vodka

1 measure chilled pineapple juice

chilled champagne or sparkling white wine

Put the pineapple and Cointreau into a mixing glass or pitcher and muddle with a spoon to crush the pineapple.

Add the vodka and pineapple juice and stir well, then strain into a glass. Fill with champagne.

Salty Dog

Serves 1

1 tbsp granulated sugar

1 tbsp coarse salt

lime wedge

6–8 ice cubes, cracked

2 measures vodka

grapefruit juice

Mix the sugar and salt in a saucer. Rub the rim of a chilled cocktail glass with the lime wedge, then dip it in the sugar-and-salt mixture to frost.

Fill the glass with cracked ice and pour the vodka over them.

Fill with grapefruit juice and stir to mix. Drink with a straw.

Flying Grasshopper

Serves 1

cracked ice

1 measure vodka

1 measure green crème de menthe

1 measure white crème de menthe

Put the cracked ice into a mixing glass or pitcher and pour in the vodka and crème de menthes. Stir well and strain into a cocktail glass.

Bullshot

Serves 1

1 measure vodka

2 measures beef consommé or good stock

dash fresh lemon juice

2 dashes Worcestershire sauce

ice

celery salt

lemon peel strip, to decorate

Shake all the liquid ingredients well with ice and strain into a glass with extra ice.

Sprinkle with celery salt and dress with the strip of lemon peel.

Cranberry Collins

Serves 1

2 measures vodka

¾ measure elderflower syrup

3 measures white cranberry and apple juice or to taste

ice

club soda

cranberries and lime slice, to decorate

Shake the vodka, elderflower syrup, and cranberry and apple juice over ice until well frosted.

Strain into a Collins glass with more ice and fill with club soda to taste.

Dress with the cranberries and the slice of lime.

Silver Berry

Serves 1

1 measure raspberry vodka, iced

1 measure creme de cassis, iced

1 measure Cointreau, iced

circle of silver paper and frozen berry, to decorate

Carefully and slowly layer the three liquors in the order listed in a well-iced shot glass or tall thin cocktail glass. They must be well iced first and may need time to settle into their layers.

Dress with the silver paper and frozen berry.

Golden Frog

Serves 1

ice cubes

1 measure vodka

1 measure Strega

1 measure Galliano

1 measure lemon juice

Blend 4–6 ice cubes in a blender with the vodka, Strega, Galliano, and lemon juice until slushy.

Pour into a chilled cocktail glass.

Fifth Avenue

Serves 1

1 measure dark crème de cacao, iced

1 measure apricot brandy, iced

1 measure cream

Pour the ingredients, one at a time, into a chilled glass. Pour the layers slowly over the back of a spoon resting against the edge of the glass. Each layer should float on top of the previous one.

Stars & Swirls

Serves 1

1 measure Malibu

large ice cube

½ measure strawberry or raspberry liqueur

1 tsp blue curaçao

Chill a small shot glass really well.

Pour in the Malibu and add a large ice cube.

Carefully pour in the strawberry liqueur and blue curaçao from opposite sides of the glass very slowly so they fall down the sides and swirl around.

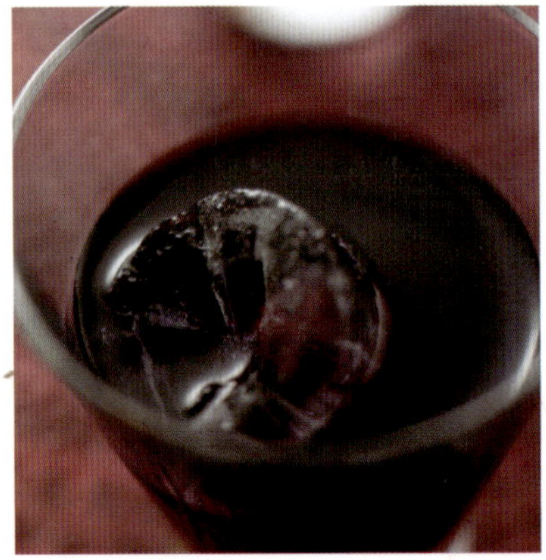

Peppermint Patty

Serves 1

cracked ice

1 measure white crème de cacao

1 measure white crème de menthe

Put the ice in a cocktail shaker and pour in the crème de cacao and crème de menthe.

Close the shaker and shake vigorously for 10–20 seconds, until the outside of the shaker is misted. Strain into a shot glass.

White Diamond Frappé

Serves 1

¼ measure peppermint schnapps
¼ measure white crème de cacao
¼ measure anise liqueur
¼ measure lemon juice
crushed ice

Shake all the liquid ingredients over ice until frosted.

Strain into a chilled shot glass and add a small spoonful of crushed ice.

Cherry Kitch

Serves 1

1 measure cherry brandy

2 measures pineapple juice

½ measure kirsch

1 egg white

crushed ice

frozen maraschino cherry, to decorate

Shake the cherry brandy, pineapple juice, kirsch, and egg white well over ice until frosted.

Pour into a chilled tall thin glass and fill with the frozen maraschino cherry.

Fancy Free

Serves 1

1/3 measure cherry brandy, iced

1/3 measure Cointreau, iced

1/3 measure apricot liqueur, iced

Pour the three liqueurs in order into an iced, tall shot glass, pouring them over the back of a spoon so they form colored layers.

Fuzzy Navel

Serves 1

2 measures vodka

1 measure peach schnapps

1 cup orange juice

cracked ice

orange slice, to decorate

Shake the vodka, peach schnapps, and orange juice vigorously over cracked ice until well frosted.

Strain into a chilled cocktail glass and dress with the orange slice.

4

For the Weekend

Bellini

Serves 1

1 measure fresh peach juice made from lightly sweetened peeled and blended peaches

confectioners' sugar

3 measures champagne, chilled

Dip the rim of a champagne flute into some peach juice and then into the sugar to create a sugar-frosted effect. Set aside to dry.

Pour the peach juice into the chilled flute.

Carefully fill with champagne.

Mudslide

Serves 1

$1\frac{1}{2}$ measures Kahlúa

$1\frac{1}{2}$ measures Baileys Irish Cream

$1\frac{1}{2}$ measures vodka

cracked ice

Shake the Kahlúa, Baileys Irish Cream, and vodka vigorously over ice until well frosted.

Strain into a chilled glass.

White Lady

Serves 1

2 measures gin
1 measure triple sec
1 measure lemon juice
cracked ice

Shake the gin, triple sec, and lemon juice vigorously over ice until well frosted.

Strain into a chilled cocktail glass.

Black Widow

Serves 1

⅔ measure dark rum

⅓ measure Southern Comfort

juice ½ lime

dash curaçao

ice

club soda

lime peel twist, to decorate

Shake the rum, Southern Comfort, lime juice, and curaçao together well over ice and strain into a chilled tumbler.

Fill with club soda to taste and dress with the twist of lime peel.

Kamikaze

Serves 1

1 measure vodka

1 measure triple sec

½ measure fresh lime juice

½ measure fresh lemon juice

ice

dry white wine, chilled

cucumber slices, to decorate

Shake the vodka, triple sec, lime juice, and lemon juice together over ice until well frosted.

Strain into a chilled glass and fill with wine.

Dress with the slices of cucumber.

White Cosmopolitan

Serves 1

$1\frac{1}{2}$ measures Limoncello

$\frac{1}{2}$ measure Cointreau

1 measure white cranberry and grape juice

ice

dash orange bitters

few red cranberries, to decorate

Shake the Limoncello, Cointreau, and cranberry and grape juice over ice until well frosted.

Strain into a chilled glass.

Add a dash of bitters and dress with the cranberries.

Indian Summer

Serves 1

1 measure vodka

2 measures Kahlúa

1 measure gin

2 measures pineapple juice

ice

tonic water

Shake the vodka, Kahlúa, gin, and pineapple juice well over ice until frosted.

Strain into a medium cocktail glass or wine glass and fill with tonic water to taste.

Deauville Passion

Serves 1

1¾ measures cognac

1¼ measures apricot Curaçao

1¼ measures passion fruit juice

ice

bitter lemon, to taste

mint leaves, to decorate

Shake the cognac, apricot Curaçao, and passion fruit juice over ice until well frosted.

Strain into a chilled glass, fill with the bitter lemon, and dress with the mint leaves.

Zombie

Serves 1

2 measures dark rum

2 measures white rum

1 measure golden rum

1 measure triple sec

1 measure lime juice

1 measure orange juice

1 measure pineapple juice

1 measure guava juice

1 tbsp grenadine

1 tbsp orgeat

1 tsp Pernod

crushed ice

fresh mint sprigs and pineapple wedges, to decorate

Shake all the liquids together over crushed ice until well combined and frosted.

Pour without straining into a chilled glass.

Dress with the mint and wedges of pineapple.

Ocean Breeze

Serves 1

1 measure white rum

1 measure amaretto

½ measure blue curaçao

½ measure pineapple juice

crushed ice

club soda

Shake the white rum, amaretto, blue curaçao, and pineapple juice together over ice.

Pour into a tall glass and fill with club soda to taste.

Pink Squirrel

Serves 1

2 measures dark crème de cacao

1 measure crème de noyaux

1 measure light cream

cracked ice

Shake the crème de cacao, crème de noyaux, and light cream vigorously over ice until well frosted.

Strain into a chilled glass.

Orange Blossom

Serves 1

2 measures gin

2 measures orange juice

cracked ice

orange slice, to decorate

Shake the gin and orange juice vigorously over ice until well frosted.

Strain into a chilled cocktail glass and dress with the orange slice.

Moonlight

Serves 4

3 measures grapefruit juice

4 measures gin

1 measure kirsch

4 measures white wine

½ tsp lemon zest

ice

Shake all the ingredients well over ice and strain into chilled glasses.

Screwdriver

Serves 1

cracked ice
2 measures vodka
orange juice
orange slice, to decorate

Fill a chilled glass with cracked ice.

Pour the vodka over the ice and fill with orange juice.

Stir well to mix and dress with the slice of orange.

Seabreeze

Serves 1

1½ measures vodka

½ measure cranberry juice

ice

pink grapefruit juice, to taste

Shake the vodka and cranberry juice over ice until frosted.

Pour into a chilled tumbler or long glass and fill with pink grapefruit juice to taste.

Blue Monday

Serves 1

cracked ice

1 measure vodka

½ measure Cointreau

1 tbsp blue curaçao

Put the cracked ice into a mixing glass or pitcher and pour in the vodka, Cointreau, and curaçao. Stir well and strain into a cocktail glass.

Moscow Mule

Serves 1

2 measures vodka

1 measure lime juice

cracked ice

ginger beer

lime slice, to decorate

Shake the vodka and lime juice vigorously over ice until well frosted.

Fill a chilled tall glass halfway with cracked ice and strain the cocktail over them.

Fill with ginger beer. Dress with the slice of lime.

Black Russian

Serves 1

2 measures vodka

1 measure coffee liqueur

4–6 ice cubes, cracked

Pour the vodka and liqueur over cracked ice in a small chilled glass.

Stir to mix.